PRAYERS
for the Road Home

Signposts for
Reclaiming Your Faith

PRAYERS
for the Road Home

Signposts for
Reclaiming Your Faith

COMPILED BY
JAC CAMPBELL, C.S.P.

Paulist Press
New York / Mahwah, N.J.

Book design by Theresa Sparacio and Lynn Else
Cover design by Lynn Else

Copyright © 2001 by The Missionary Society
of St. Paul the Apostle in the State of New York

Library of Congress Cataloging-in-Publication Data

Prayers for the road home : signposts for reclaiming
your faith / compiled by Jac Campbell.
p. cm.
ISBN 0-8091-4004-7 (alk. paper)
1. Catholic Church—Prayer-books and devotions—English.
2. Ex-church members—Prayer-books and devotions—
English. I. Campbell, Jac.

BX2130 .P75 2001
242′.802—dc21
2001016306

Published by Paulist Press
997 Macarthur Boulevard
Mahwah, New Jersey 07430

www.paulistpress.com

Printed and bound in the
United States of America

Prayer Themes in the Text

v

Permissions

Introduction

Prayers for the Road Home is a collection of traditional and contemporary prayers, poems and reflections intended as a useful companion for those of us who may be rediscovering the church as a place to call home. Whatever our past experiences with family or church, we yearn for "home" not only as a place of shelter but also as a source of nourishment, companionship and life. In the home each of us seeks, we learn where we came from and come to discover where we are heading. From home we reenter the world each day, renewed and strengthened to face the challenges life provides.

This small book was written with the presumption that the church offers a home where we can discover at the center a God who is, by definition, love. It was developed out of the gentle ministry of Father Jac Campbell, C.S.P. From his home base in Boston, Father Jac created *Landings*, a program for reaching out to inactive Catholics and welcoming those who seek to return to an active life in the church. In parishes throughout the United States, *Landings* groups provide a place of hospitality where returning Catholics gather with parishioners to pray, share faith and discuss Catholic spirituality. These groups came to see the value of having a collection of prayers to support them on their journey. While this selection can be used with profit by any Catholic, it is especially designed for the benefit of those who may be returning, or considering returning, to the church.

It is challenging to be a Christian in today's world, but faith brings a joy that can persist through trial and ambiguity. God's word to us is one of encouragement. Our response is thanksgiving and praise. This is what we discover in prayer.

There are many ways to pray. Some of us have discovered the benefit of quiet prayer or meditation, which is sometimes called a "prayer of the heart." We don't always require words to place ourselves in God's presence. Yet most of us need words, at least some of the time, to give voice to our deepest desires. Our Catholic tradition provides a wealth of written and spoken prayers, many of which have been passed down through generations of ordinary faithful people. Here are some of the most beloved.

This book is divided into sections, each taking for its heading a theme drawn from an aspect of Catholic belief or practice. The sections with the themes "God" through "Holy Spirit" provide prayers for the different ways we come to know God—as mystery and creator, as compassionate, self-giving love embodied in the human person of Jesus, and as a holy Spirit present wherever a sinful church is transformed into a community of faith, hope and love. The sections with the themes "Baptism-Community" through "Sin and Forgiveness" offer prayers drawn from the ways we experience God as alive and with us. Through immersion in the waters of Baptism we become members of the church. Through sharing in the Eucharist (a Greek word meaning "prayer of thanksgiving") we receive the bread and wine Catholics encounter as the living presence of Christ, and through the experience of forgiving and being forgiven God frees us from the burdens of our past. The sections with the themes "Marriage and Family" through "Heaven and Earth, Death and Resurrection" present prayers that are part of our experience of God outside and beyond the walls of a church: in the small community of marriage and family, in moments of personal change, growth and ordinary daily living, and in our encounter with life's ultimate realities, death and what hope calls us to beyond death. The section entitled "Home" provides some of the traditional prayers that we remember from our childhood. Not all will speak the voice of our own heart. But some may.

Many of the prayers in this collection are taken from the *Sacramentary*. This is a book that contains the prayers for the daily celebration of the Eucharist (also known by many Catholics as the Mass). It is the daily community prayer of the church. There are in particular selections from the "Prefaces" to the Eucharistic

3

Prayer. In the Mass, these are introductions to the main prayer of thanksgiving. There are nearly one hundred Prefaces in the *Sacramentary*, each dealing with a particular theme connected with a season or feast day of the church year. Yet all express an invitation to praise and give thanks for the goodness of God. When you pray these prayers, you are in a special way praying "with" other Christians throughout the world. (You will note that, while inclusive language is observed as much as possible in the text, the original wording of these liturgical texts is retained.)

In addition to these traditional prayers, *Prayers for the Road Home* contains the words of contemporary people of faith and prayer. Their poems and musings struggle to express, often with eloquence, an experience of the spirit that must somehow remain always beyond expression. Some of their thoughts may surprise or delight you, or lead you to understand God and God's dealings with the world in a way you hadn't thought about before. We invite you to browse through them as if sorting through a chest of family treasures, perhaps setting aside some for the moment but discovering in others a source of inspiration and an incentive to your prayer.

God

You Are Near

Yahweh, I know you are near
Standing always at my side.
You guard me from the foes,
And you lead me in ways everlasting.

DANIEL L. SCHUTTE, S.J.

Embracing Life's Challenges

There are times when our image of God seems to shatter, and it feels as if our faith is fading. St. John of the Cross encourages us to embrace those moments. Since no human concept or idea can contain God, he claims these are graced moments of growth, times to discard what is outdated and embrace the next gift of understanding and faith.

A nun taught me the same lesson in the third grade: "Young man, your stomach is not large enough to hold an elephant. Your mind will never be large enough to contain God. So relax."

JAC CAMPBELL

Seeing with the Heart

And now here is my secret, a very simple secret: It is
only with the heart that one can see rightly; what is
essential is invisible to the eye.

ANTOINE DE SAINT-EXUPERY

God's Care

If God is for us, who is against us? He who did not withhold his own Son, but gave him up for all of us, will he not with him also give us everything else? Who will bring any charge against God's elect? It is God who justifies. Who is to condemn? It is Christ Jesus, who died, yes, who was raised, who is at the right hand of God, who indeed intercedes for us.

ROMANS 8:31B–34

Trinity

Indeed it is deserving, just and right
And salutary, for us everywhere
And always, that we thank you, holy Lord,
Almighty Father and eternal God.
Together with your sole-begotten Son
And Holy Spirit, you are Lord and God;
Not one in single personality,
But one in essence while in persons three.
For what, yourself revealing, we believe
About your glory, that we also hold
With neither difference nor disparity,
Of Son and Holy Spirit—three in one.
Confessing true, eternal Deity
While holding its essential unity,
We worship still each Person as himself,
And equal to each in majesty.

From the PREFACE FOR THE TRINITY

A God without Names

For Eve and Adam
God was a mystery
Lodged at the end of innocence.
Pain opened a path to birth,
Love revealed its sweetness
In the shadow of death's demand.

Abraham's God brought risk,
Unsought invitations,
Shedding the safe and certain
For an unknown future
In a foreign land.

Sarah's God dwelled in laughter,
Teasing with surprises usually unsettling,
Sometimes life-giving.

Consider Joseph,
Falling from beloved child
To slave and criminal.
Rising from pit to throne
As Pharaoh's governor.
Where was God
In his strange journey?
Perhaps in the falling and the rising,

More in his heart's homeward turn
The moment he forgave his brothers.

Moses saw only the back of God.
A shadow
Whose very name was an evasion,
A whirlwind he could not control
And struggled to explain,
Yet whose promises were true.

Jeremiah hoped he followed God
By speaking an unwelcome truth
And suffering for it.
Hosea's God emerged
In faithfulness beyond all reason.
Esther, risking her privileged place
To plead for those who had no voice,
Did she realize
The words she spoke were God's?

I turn to scripture
Searching for answers,
For God,
In the stories of old believers.
But the God they tried to know
Is not so different
From the One who haunts my ordinary life.
Who
Seldom answers door knocks,
And appears more in questions than answers.

The mystery I pursue eludes me,
A glimpse of someone's back
Vanishing around a corner
Just as I close the distance between us,
And then showing up,
when I've ceased to look,
in a homeless person's raging truth,
in an aged woman's ravaged dignity,
in a new start after a bad fall.

JOSEPH SCOTT, C.S.P.

God Does Not Abandon Us

But Zion said, "The LORD has forsaken me;
   my LORD has forgotten me."
Can a woman forget her nursing child,
or show no compassion for the child of her womb?
Even these may forget,
   yet I will not forget you,
See, I have inscribed you on the palms of my hands....

ISAIAH 49:14–16A

Nothing Can Separate Us from God

I am convinced that neither death nor life, nor angels, nor rulers, nor things present, nor things to come, nor powers, nor height, nor depth, nor anything else in all creation, will be able to separate us from the love of God in Christ Jesus our Lord.

ROMANS 8:38–39

Comfort in God's Care

Comfort, O comfort my people,
says your God.
Speak tenderly to Jerusalem,
and cry to her
That she has served her term,
That her penalty is paid,
That she has received from the LORD'S hand
double for all her sins....
See, the LORD GOD comes with might,
and his arm rules for him;
his reward is with him,
and his recompense before him.
He will feed his flock like a shepherd;
he will gather the lambs in his arms,
and carry them in his bosom,
and gently lead the mother sheep.

ISAIAH 40:1–2, 10–11

Jesus

Tidings of Great Joy

His future coming was proclaimed by all the
      prophets.
The virgin mother bore him in her womb
with love beyond all telling.
John the Baptist was his herald
and made him known when at last he came.

In his love Christ has filled us with joy
as we prepare to celebrate his birth,
so that when he comes he may find us watching in
      prayer,
our hearts filled with wonder and praise.

From a PREFACE FOR ADVENT

God Becomes Flesh

In the wonder of the incarnation
your eternal Word has brought to the eyes of faith
a new and radiant vision of your glory.
In him we see our God made visible
and so are caught up in love of the God we cannot
 see.

From a PREFACE FOR CHRISTMAS

Recognizing Christ in Christmas

Today you fill our hearts with joy
as we recognize in Christ the revelation of your love.
No eye can see his glory as our God,
yet now he is seen as one like us.

Christ is your Son before all ages,
yet now he is born in time.
He has come to lift up all things to himself,
to restore unity to creation,
and to lead humankind from exile into your heavenly
     kingdom.

With all the angels of heaven
we sing our joyful hymn of praise....

From a PREFACE FOR CHRISTMAS

Christ Is for All People

Today you revealed in Christ your eternal plan of
        salvation
and showed him as the light of all peoples.
Now that his glory has shone among us
you have renewed humanity in his immortal image.

Now with angels and archangels,
and the whole company of heaven,
we sing the unending hymn of your praise....

> From the PREFACE FOR THE
> FEAST OF THE EPIPHANY

Living Lent

Each year you give us this joyful season
when we prepare to celebrate the paschal mystery
with heart and mind renewed.
You give us a spirit of loving reverence for you, our
        Father,
and of willing service to our neighbor.

As we recall the great events that gave us new life in
        Christ,
you bring the image of your Son to perfection within
        us.

Now, with angels and archangels,
and the whole company of heaven,
    we sing the unending hymn of your praise....

From a PREFACE FOR LENT

Prayer before a Crucifix

O good and gentle Jesus look upon me,
As falling on my knees before your face,
I beg you and implore with soul afire
To fix within my heart a lively sense
Of faith, hope, love, contrition for my sins,
With steadfast purpose to amend my life.
The while with deepest love and grief of soul
I contemplate and ponder in my heart
Your five most precious wounds, and call to mind
What David, O good Jesus, spoke of you:
My enemies have pierced my hands and feet,
And I can number all my bones. Amen.

Easter Hymn

Light's glittering morn bedecks the sky,
Heav'n thunders forth its victor cry,
The glad earth shouts its triumph high
And groaning hell makes wild reply.

While he, the King of glorious might,
Treads down death's strength in death's despite,
And trampling hell by victor's right
Brings forth his sleeping saints to light.
Hell's pains are loosed and tears are fled.
Captivity is captive led:
The angel crowned with light has said:
"The Lord is risen from the dead!"

To God the Father let us sing.
To God the Son our risen King.
And equally let us adore
The Spirit, God forevermore.

The Joy of Easter

We praise you with greater joy than ever
in this Easter season,
when Christ became our paschal sacrifice.
In him a new age has dawned,
the long reign of sin is ended,
a broken world has been renewed,
and we are once again made whole.

The joy of the resurrection renews the whole world,
while the choirs of heaven sing for ever to your
      glory....

From a PREFACE FOR EASTER

An Open Heart

He told me one time he forgot
himself and his heart
opened up like a door
        with a loose latch
and he tried for days to put
        it all back in proper
                order
        but finally gave up
    and left it all jumbled up there
in a pile and loved everything equally.

BRIAN ANDREAS

Soul of Christ

Soul of Christ, be my sanctification
Body of Christ, be my salvation;
Blood of Christ, fill all my veins;
Water of Christ's side, wash out my stains;
Passion of Christ, my comfort be;
O good Jesu, listen to me:
In the wounds I fain would hide,
Ne'er to be parted from thy side;
Guard me, should the foe assail me;
Call me when my life shall fail me;
Bid me come to thee above,
With thy saints to sing thy love
World without end. Amen.

TRANSLATION OF A TRADITIONAL
LATIN PRAYER, "ANIMA CHRISTI"

Holy Spirit

The Gift of the Holy Spirit

You give your gifts of grace for every time and season,
as you guide the church
in the marvelous ways of your providence.

You give us your Holy Spirit
to help us always by his power,
so that with loving trust
we may turn to you in all our troubles,
and give you thanks in all our joys,
through Jesus Christ our Lord.

In our joy we sing to your glory
with the choirs of angels....

From a PREFACE FOR THE HOLY SPIRIT

Come, Holy Ghost

1. Come, Holy Ghost, Creator blest,
And in our hearts take up your rest.
Come with your grace and heav'nly aid,
To fill the hearts which you have made,
To fill the hearts which you have made.

2. O Comforter, to you we cry,
The heav'nly gift of God most high;
The fount of life and fire of love,
And sweet anointing from above,
And sweet anointing from above.

3. To ev'ry sense your light impart,
And shed your love in ev'ry heart.
To our weak flesh your strength supply:
Unfailing courage from on high,
Unfailing courage from on high.

4. O grant that we through you may come
To know the Father and the Son,
And hold with firm, unchanging faith
That you are Spirit of them both,
That you are Spirit of them both.

5. Now let us praise Father and Son,
And Holy Spirit, with them one;
And may the Son on us bestow
The gifts that from the Spirit flow,
The gifts that from the Spirit flow.

Come, Thou Holy Spirit

Come, thou Holy Spirit, come!
And from thy celestial home
Shed a ray of light divine!

Come, thou Father of the poor!
Come thou source of all our store!
Come, within our bosoms shine!

Thou, of comforters the best;
Thou, the soul's most welcome guest;
Sweet refreshment here below.

In our labor, rest most sweet;
Grateful coolness in the heat;
Solace in the midst of woe.

O most blessed Light divine,
Shine within these hearts of thine,
And our inmost being fill!

Where thou are not, we have naught,
Nothing good in deed or thought,
Nothing free from taint of ill.

Heal our wounds, our strength renew;
On our dryness pour thy dew;
Wash the stains of guilt away.

Bend the stubborn heart and will;
Melt the frozen, warm the chill;
Guide the steps that go astray.

TRANSLATION OF A TRADITIONAL LATIN
HYMN, "VENI SANCTE SPIRITUS"

Prayer to the Holy Spirit

Holy Spirit, Lord of light,
From the clear celestial height
Thy pure beaming radiance give.

Come, thou Father of the poor,
Come with treasures that endure,
Come, thou light of all that live.

Bend the stubborn heart and will
Melt the frozen, warm the chill,
Guide the steps that go astray.

Give us comfort when we die,
Give us life with thee on high,
Give us joys that never end.

"BEFORE MASS, NO. 56," From
THE NEW ST. BASIL HYMNAL

A Prayer for Unity among Christians

Through Christ you bring us to the knowledge of
      your truth,
that we may be united by one faith and one baptism
to become his body.
Through Christ you have given the Holy Spirit to all
      peoples.

How wonderful are the works of the Spirit,
revealed in so many gifts!
Yet how marvelous is the unity
the Spirit creates from their diversity,
as he dwells in the hearts of your children
filling the whole church with his presence
and guiding it with his wisdom!

In our joy we sing to your glory
with all the choirs of angels....

From the PREFACE FOR CHRISTIAN UNITY

Baptism—
Community

Gather Us In

Gather us in and hold us forever,
Gather us in and make us your own,
Gather us in, all people together,
Fire of love in our flesh and our bone.

MARTY HAUGEN

Christ's Body

Christ has no body now on earth but yours;
yours are the only hands with which he can do his
     work,
yours are the only feet with which he can go about the
     world,
yours are the only eyes through which his compassion
can shine forth upon a troubled world.
Christ has no body on earth now but yours.

TERESA OF AVILA

Giving Thanks for the Saints

You are glorified in your saints,
for their glory is the crowning of your gifts.
In their lives on earth
you give us an example.
In our communion with them,
you give us their friendship.
In their prayer for the Church
you give us strength and protection.
This great company of witnesses spurs us on to
         victory,
to share their prize of everlasting glory,
through Jesus Christ our Lord.

With angels and archangels
and the whole company of saints
we sing our unending hymn of praise….

From a PREFACE FOR HOLY
MEN AND WOMEN

Faithfulness, Not Performance

My Lord God, I have no idea where I am going.
I do not see the road ahead of me.
I cannot know for certain where it will end.
Nor do I really know myself,
and the fact that I think I am following your will
does not mean that I am actually doing so.
But I believe that the desire to please you does in fact
     please you.
And I hope I have that desire in all that I am doing.
I hope that I will never do anything apart from that
     desire.
And I know that if I do this you will lead me by the
     right road,
though I may know nothing about it.
Therefore I will trust you always
though I may seem to be lost and in the shadow of
     death.
I will not fear, for you are ever with me,
and you will not leave me to face my perils alone.

THOMAS MERTON

Prayer for Guidance

I am not asking you tonight, Lord, for time to do this
    and then that,
but your grace to do conscientiously, in the time that
    you give me,
what you want me to do.

MICHEL QUOIST

Prayer When Visiting a Church

We thank you now for this house of prayer
in which you bless your family
as we come to you on pilgrimage.

Here you reveal your presence
by sacramental signs,
and make us one with you
through the unseen bond of grace.
Here you build your temple of living stones,
and bring the Church to its full stature
as the body of Christ throughout the world,
to reach its perfection at last
in the heavenly city of Jerusalem,
which is the vision of your peace.

In communion with all the angels and saints
we bless and praise your greatness
in the temple of your glory....

From a PREFACE FOR THE
DEDICATION OF A CHURCH

Inner Awareness

I pray…so that, with the eyes of your heart
    enlightened,
you may know what is the hope
to which he has called you….

EPHESIANS 1:18

Eucharist

God's Mercy Is without Limit

If we do not pray, it is because we sometimes hold superstitions, one form being this: if I give myself up too much to God, God will give me something too hard which I cannot do. This is not Christian maturity. It presupposes that Our Lord is playing tricks with us all the time. We have to get rid of the thought that God is a powerful deceiver, that God is ready to catch us in some moment of weakness and impose some terrible punishment. This is a dreadful concept of God. The first thing necessary is to root out every vestige of this thought of God. Don't think God is trying to catch you....

Open yourself to God. God will never, never fail us. We have to really believe we are totally forgiven. Don't set limits to the mercy of God. Don't believe that because you are not pleasing to yourself you are not pleasing to God. God does not ask for results. God asks for love.

THOMAS MERTON

Prayer for Peace

Lord, make me an instrument of your peace:
    where there is hatred, let me sow love;
    where there is injury, pardon;
    where there is doubt, faith;
    where there is despair, hope;
    where there is darkness, light;
    where there is sadness, joy.
O Divine Master, grant that I may not so much seek
    to be consoled as to console,
    to be understood as to understand,
    to be loved as to love.
For it is in giving that we receive,
    it is in pardoning that we are pardoned,
    and it is in dying that we are born to eternal life.

ATTRIBUTED TO ST. FRANCIS OF ASSISI

Wonder in the Presence of God

Godhead here in hiding, whom I do adore
Masked by these bare shadows, shape and nothing
  more.
See, Lord at thy service low lies here a heart
Lost, all lost in wonder at the God thou art.

Seeing, touching, tasting are in thee deceived;
How says trusting hearing? That shall be believed:
What God's Son has told me, take for truth I do;
Truth himself speaks truly or there's nothing true.

O thou, our reminder of Christ crucified,
Living Bread the life of us for whom he died,
Lend this life to me then: feed and feast my mind,
There be thou the sweetness we were meant to find.

Jesus whom I look at shrouded here below,
I beseech thee send me what I thirst for so,
Some day to gaze on thee face to face in light
And be blest for ever with thy glory's sight.

TRANSLATION OF A HYMN BY THOMAS
AQUINAS, "ADORO TE" ("I ADORE YOU")

The Food of Life

At the last supper,
as he sat at table with his apostles,
he offered himself to you as the spotless lamb,
the acceptable gift that gives you perfect praise.
Christ has given us this memorial of his passion
to bring us its saving power until the end of time.

In this great sacrament you feed your people
and strengthen them in holiness
so that the family of humankind
may come to walk in the light of one faith,
in one communion of love.
We come then to this wonderful sacrament
to be fed at your table
and grow into the likeness of the risen Christ.

Earth unites with heaven
to sing the new song of creation
as we adore and praise you for ever....

From a PREFACE FOR THE HOLY EUCHARIST

Peace Is Flowing Like a River

Peace is flowing like a river,
Flowing out of you and me.
Flowing out into the desert,
Setting all the captives free.

God's love is flowing like a river,
Flowing out of you and me.
Flowing out into the desert,
Setting all the captives free.

Alleluia, alleluia…
Flowing out of you and me.
Flowing out into the desert,
Setting all the captives free.

God's peace is flowing like a river,
Flowing out of you and me.
Flowing out into the desert,
Setting all the captives free.

CAREY LANDRY

Recognizing Christ in the Breaking of the Bread

Now on that same day two of them were going to a village named Emmaus, about seven miles from Jerusalem, and talking with each other about all these things that had happened. While they were talking and discussing, Jesus himself came near and went with them, but their eyes were kept from recognizing him....As they came near the village to which they were going, he walked ahead as if he were going on. But they urged him strongly, saying, "Stay with us, because it is almost evening and the day is now nearly over." So he went in to stay with them. When he was at the table with them, he took bread, blessed and broke it, and gave it to them. Then their eyes were opened, and they recognized him....

LUKE 24:13–16, 28–31A

Traditional Hymn before the Eucharist

Down in adoration falling,
Lo! the sacred Host we hail.
Lo! o'er ancient forms departing,
Newer rites of grace prevail.
Faith for all defects supplying,
Where the feeble senses fail.

To the everlasting Father
And the Son who reigns on high,
With the Spirit still proceeding
Age to age eternally,
Be salvation, honor, blessing,
Might and endless majesty. Amen.

TRANSLATED FROM THE LATIN HYMN
"TANTUM ERGO"

Prayer of Silence

In silence,
To be there before you, Lord, that's all,
To shut the eyes of my body,
To shut the eyes of my soul,
And to be still and silent,
To expose myself to you who are there,
    exposed to me.
To be there before you,
    the eternal presence....

MICHEL QUOIST

Sin and Forgiveness

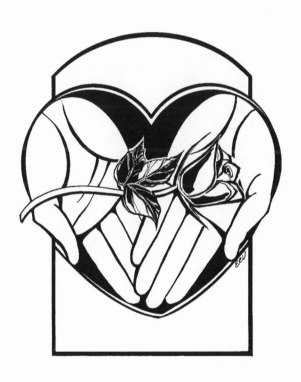

Forgiveness

God forgives you.
forgive others:
forgive yourself.

From *A NEW ZEALAND PRAYER BOOK*

Love without Judgment

The scribes and the Pharisees brought a woman who had been caught in adultery; and making her stand before all of them, they said to him, "Teacher, this woman was caught in the very act of committing adultery. Now in the law Moses commanded us to stone such women. Now what do you say?" They said this to test him, so that they might have some charge to bring against him. Jesus bent down and wrote with his finger on the ground.

When they kept on questioning him, he straightened up and said to them, "Let anyone among you who is without sin be the first to throw a stone at her." And once again he bent down and wrote on the ground. When they heard it, they went away, one by one, beginning with the elders, and Jesus was left alone with the woman standing before him.

Jesus straightened up and said to her, "Woman, where are they? Has no one condemned you?" She said, "No one, sir." And Jesus said, "Neither do I condemn you. Go your way, and from now on do not sin again."

JOHN 8:3–11

Sorrow for Sin

O my God, I am heartily sorry
for having offended You,
    and I detest all my sins,
because I dread the loss of heaven
    and the pains of hell,
but most of all because
    they offend You, my God,
Who are all-good
    and deserving of all my love.
I firmly resolve,
    with the help of Your grace,
To confess my sins,
    to do penance,
and to amend my life. Amen.

TRADITIONAL ACT OF CONTRITION FOR SINS

The Spirit of Reconciliation

In the midst of conflict and division,
we know it is you
who turns our minds to thoughts of peace.
Your Spirit changes our hearts:
enemies begin to speak to one another,
those who were estranged join hands in friendship,
and nations seek the way of peace together.

Your Spirit is at work
when understanding puts an end to strife,
when hatred is quenched by mercy,
and vengeance gives way to forgiveness.

For this we should never cease
to thank and praise you.
We join with all the choirs of heaven
   as they sing forever to your glory....

        PREFACE FOR THE EUCHARISTIC PRAYER
          FOR MASSES OF RECONCILIATION

Amazing Grace!

Amazing grace! How sweet the sound,
That saved and strengthened me!
I once was lost, but now I'm found,
Was blind, but now I see.

'Twas grace that taught my heart to fear,
And grace my fears relieved:
How precious did that grace appear
The hour I first believed!

The Lord has promised good to me,
His word my hope secures;
He will my shield and portion be
As long as life endures.

Through many dangers, toils and snares,
I have already come;
'Tis grace hath brought me safe thus far,
and grace will lead me home.

JOHN NEWTON

Freedom

1. The Master answered and said,
"Once there lived a village
of creatures along the bottom
of a great crystal river.

2. "The current of the river
swept silently over them all—
young and old, rich and poor,
good and evil,
the current going its own way,
knowing only its own crystal self.

3. "Each creature in its own manner
clung tightly to the twigs and rocks
of the river bottom, for clinging was their way of life,
and resisting the current what each had learned
from birth.

4. "But one creature said at last, 'I am tired of clinging.
Though I cannot see it with my eyes,
I trust that the current knows
where it is going. I shall let go,
and let it take me where it will.
Clinging, I shall die of boredom.'

5. "The other creatures laughed and said,
'Fool! Let go, and that current you worship
will throw you tumbled and smashed across the rocks,
and you will die quicker than boredom!'

6. "But the one heeded them not,
and taking a breath did let go,
and at once was tumbled and smashed
by the current across the rocks.

7. "Yet in time, as the creature
refused to cling again,
the current lifted him free from the bottom,
and he was bruised and hurt no more.

8. "And the creatures downstream,
to whom he was a stranger,
cried, 'See a miracle! A creature
like ourselves, yet he flies!
See the Messiah, come to save us all!'

9. "And the one carried in the current said,
'I am no more Messiah than you.
The river delights to lift us free,
If only we dare let go.
Our true work is this voyage,
This adventure.'"

RICHARD BACH

<u>Now</u> Is the Time

God,
I spend so much time reliving yesterday
Or anticipating tomorrow
That I lose sight of the only time
That is really mine—the present.

Remind me that the past—
with its successes and failures—
is over.

I can make amends
where I have hurt others or let them down
but I can't undo what has been done.

The future is yet to be
and eagerness or apprehension
will not hasten it—or postpone it.

You give me today, one minute at a time,
that's all I have—all I ever will.

Give me the faith that knows
that each moment
contains exactly what is best for me.

Give me the hope
that trusts you enough
to forget past sins and future trials.

Give me the love
that makes each minute of life
an anticipation of eternity with you.
Amen.

A CHRISTOPHER PRAYER

Marriage and Family

Risking

ride a wild horse
with purple wings
striped yellow and black
except his head
which must be red

ride a wild horse
against the sky
hold tight to his wings
before you die
whatever else you leave
undone
once ride a wild horse
into the sun.

ANONYMOUS

Celebrating the Meaning of Marriage

You created man in love to share your divine life.
We see his high destiny in the love of husband and
      wife,
which bears the imprint of your own divine love.
Love is man's origin,
love is his constant calling,
love is his fulfillment in heaven.

The love of man and woman
is made holy in the sacrament of marriage,
and becomes the mirror of your everlasting love.
Through Christ the choirs of angels
and all the saints
praise and worship your glory.
May our voices blend with theirs
    as we join in their unending hymn....

From the PREFACE FOR MARRIAGE

A Prayer of Thanksgiving

We thank you for all that is beautiful in the world
and for the happiness you have given us.
We praise you for daylight
and for your word which lights up our minds.
We praise you for the earth,
and all the people who live on it,
and for our life which comes from you.
We know that you are good,
You love us and do great things for us.

PREFACE FOR THE EUCHARISTIC PRAYER
FOR MASSES WITH CHILDREN

The Witness of the Saints

You renew the Church in every age
by raising up men and women outstanding in
      holiness,
living witnesses of your unchanging love.
They inspire us by their heroic lives,
and help us by their constant prayers
to be the living sign of your saving power.

We praise you, Lord, with all the angels and saints
in their song of joy....

From a PREFACE FOR HOLY
MEN AND WOMEN

Self and Growth

The Meaning of Life

Life is a gift
to be opened, shared
and joyed in.
Life is not
a test to be taken.

JAC CAMPBELL

Prayer for Serenity

God,
grant me
the serenity to accept the things I cannot change,
courage to change the things that I can,
and wisdom to know the difference.
Living one day at a time,
enjoying one moment at a time;
accepting hardship as a pathway to peace;
taking, as Jesus did, this sinful world as it is,
not as I would have it:
trusting that You will make all things right
if I surrender to Your will,
so that I may be reasonably happy in this life
and supremely happy with You forever in the next.

REINHOLD NIEBUHR

Let Nothing Trouble You

Let nothing trouble you,
Let nothing scare you,
All is fleeting.
God alone is unchanging.
Patience
Everything obtains.
Who possesses God
Nothing wants.
God alone suffices.

TERESA OF AVILA ("NADA TE TURBE")

The Communion of All the Saints

Today we keep the festival of your holy city,
the heavenly Jerusalem, our mother.
Around your throne
the saints, our brothers and sisters,
sing your praise for ever.
Their glory fills us with joy,
and their communion with us in your Church
gives us inspiration and strength
as we hasten on our pilgrimage of faith,
eager to meet them.

With the great company and all the angels
we praise your glory
as we cry out with one voice....

From the PREFACE FOR THE
FEAST OF ALL SAINTS

The Apostles, Our Protectors and Guides

You are the eternal Shepherd
who never leaves his flock untended.
Through the apostles
you watch over us and protect us always.
You made them shepherds of the flock
to share in the work of your son,
and from their place in heaven they guide us still.

And so, with all the choirs of angels in heaven
we proclaim your glory
and join in their unending hymn of praise....

From the PREFACE FOR THE
FEASTS OF THE APOSTLES

A Reflection on Doing God's Work

God has created me to do Him some definite service;

He has committed some work to me which He has not committed to another.

I have my mission—I never may know it in this life, but I shall be told it in the next.

Somehow I am necessary for His purposes....I am a link in a chain, a bond of connection between persons. He has not created me for naught. I shall do good, I shall do His work; I shall be an angel of peace, a preacher of truth in my own place, while not intending it, if I do but keep His commandments and serve Him in my calling.

Therefore, I will trust Him. Whatever, wherever I am, I can never be thrown away. If I am in sickness, my sickness may serve Him; in perplexity, my perplexity may serve Him; if I am in sorrow, my sorrow may serve Him. My sickness, or perplexity, or sorrow may be necessary causes of some great end, which is quite beyond us. He does nothing in vain; He may prolong my life, He may shorten it; He knows what He is about. He may take away my friends, He may throw me among strangers, He may make me feel desolate, make my spirits sink, hide the future from me—still He knows what He is about.

JOHN HENRY NEWMAN

Pray Always

The Christian prays while walking,
while talking, while resting,
while working or reading.

CLEMENT OF ALEXANDRIA

Heaven and Earth, Death and Resurrection

For the Angels

In praising our faithful angels and archangels,
we also praise your glory,
for in honoring them, we honor you, their creator.
Their splendor shows us your greatness,
which surpasses in goodness the whole of creation.
Through Christ our Lord
the great army of angels rejoices in your glory,
in adoration and joy
we make their hymn of praise our own....

From the PREFACE FOR THE ANGELS

The Dead Will Rise

For the Lord himself, with a cry of command, with the archangel's call and with the sound of God's trumpet, will descend from heaven, and the dead in Christ will rise first. Then we who are alive, who are left, will be caught up in the clouds together with them to meet the Lord in the air; and so we will be with the Lord forever. Therefore encourage one another with these words.

1 THESSALONIANS 4:16–18

Prayer of Thanksgiving

O God, thank you for the Resurrection!
Thank you for reunion,
   and reconciliation.
I praise you.
I love you.
I worship you! Forever and ever! Amen.

The Strife Is O'er

Refrain: Alleluia! Alleluia! Alleluia!

The strife is o'er, the battle won, the victory of life is
      won;
The song of triumph has begun: Alleluia!

Refrain

The three sad days have quickly sped;
He rises glorious from the dead:
All glory to our risen Head!
Alleluia!

Refrain

Lord, by the stripes which wounded thee,
From death's dread sting thy servants free,
That we may live and sing to thee: Alleluia!

Refrain

The Dead

Indeed, it is deserving, just and right
And salutary, for us everywhere
And always, that we thank you, holy Lord,
Almighty Father and eternal God,
Through Christ our Lord.
Through him has dawned for us the blessed hope
Of resurrection; saddened though we be
By certainty that death is on its way,
We still have promise of a future life.
Concerning then your faithful, life, O Lord,
Is changed and never brought to final end.
For when their earthly dwelling place dissolves
Eternal mansions beckon from above.
And there with Angels and Archangels, Thrones,
Dominions and all heaven's warrior hosts
Our voices rise in endless praise and sing:
Holy....

BASIL DOYLE, C.S.P.

Farewell to One Who Has Died

Before we go our separate ways,
let us take leave of our brother/sister.
May our farewell express our affection for him/her;
may it ease our sadness and strengthen our hope.
One day we shall joyfully greet him/her again
when the love of Christ, which conquers all things,
destroys even death itself.

Trusting in God,
we have prayed together for N.
and now we come to the last farewell.
There is sadness in parting,
but we take comfort in the hope
that one day we shall see N. again
and enjoy his/her friendship.
Although this congregation will disperse in sorrow,
the mercy of God will gather us together again
in the joy of his kingdom.
Therefore let us console one another
in the faith of Jesus Christ.

From *THE ORDER OF CHRISTIAN FUNERALS*

In Hope of the Resurrection

May Saints and angels lead you on,
Escorting you where Christ has gone.
Now he has called you, come to him
Who sits above the seraphim.

Come to the peace of Abraham
And come to the supper of the Lamb:
Come to the glory of the blessed,
And to perpetual light and rest.

Based on "IN PARADISUM"

After a Death

Saints of God, come to his/her aid!
Come to meet him/her, angels of the Lord!

May Christ, who called you, take you to himself;
May angels lead you to Abraham's side.

Give him/her eternal rest, O Lord,
And may your light shine upon him/her forever.

From *THE ORDER OF CHRISTIAN FUNERALS*

Other Devotions, Reflections and Traditional Prayers

Devotion to the Saints Today

Like all of our Catholic devotions, devotion to the saints has changed significantly since the Second Vatican Council. To discourage exaggerated practices of this devotion in isolation from the church's teachings, veneration of the saints—according to the *Dogmatic Constitution on the Church*—has been tied in more closely with worship of Christ and with the liturgical life of the Church:

Every authentic witness of love, indeed, offered by us to those who are in heaven tends to and terminates in Christ, "the crown of all saints," and through him in God who is wonderful in his saints and is glorified in them.

It is especially in the sacred liturgy that our union with the heavenly Church is best realized: in the liturgy, through sacramental signs, the power of the Holy Spirit acts on us, and with community rejoicing we celebrate together the praise of the divine majesty....When, then, we celebrate the eucharistic sacrifice we are most closely united to the worship of the heavenly Church: when in the fellowship of communion we honor and remember the glorious

101

Mary ever virgin, St. Joseph, the holy apostles and martyrs and all the saints.

DOGMATIC CONSTITUTION
ON THE CHURCH, NO. 50

The Gift of the Saints

And consequently, it is not possible to set limits to the comprehensiveness and effectiveness of this open circle.

There is perhaps no more comforting truth about the church than that in it there is a community, a communion of saints. For, on the one hand, this means that there is a continually overflowing richness on which all the poor may draw; it is also called the treasure of the church. It is precisely the same as the incalculable fruitfulness of those who offer themselves and all that they have to God to dispose of for the sake of the brotherhood and sisterhood. Real power goes forth from them; they are not spared by love (Romans 8:32) but are rigorously shared....This excess which comes to us makes us poor and humble, for we sense precisely that we can only draw on such richness in the same spirit in which it has been given....The idea of the communion of saints inspires no little caution in us. On the other hand, it also exhorts us not to underestimate the fruitfulness which has been given us by God.

HANS URS VON BALTHASAR

What Makes a Saint?

Only God makes saints. Still, it is up to us to tell their stories. That, in the end, is the only rationale for the process of "making saints." What sort of story befits a saint? Not tragedy, certainly. Comedy comes closer to capturing the playfulness of genuine holiness and the supreme logic of a life lived in and through God. An element of suspense is also required: until the story is over, one can never be certain of the outcome. True saints are the last people on earth to presume their own salvation—in this life or in the next.

My own hunch is that the story of a saint is always a love story. It is the story of a God who loves, and of the beloved who learns how to reciprocate and share that "harsh and dreadful love."

It is a story that includes misunderstanding, deception, betrayal, concealment, reversal and revelation of character. It is, if the saints are to be trusted, our story. But to be a saint is not to be a solitary lover. It is to enter into deeper communion with everyone and everything that exists.

KENNETH L. WOODWARD

Prayer to the Blessed Mother

Remember, O most gracious Virgin Mary,
that never was it known
That anyone who fled to your protection,
implored your help,
or sought your intercession was left unaided.
Inspired by this confidence,
I fly unto you,
O Virgin of virgins, my Mother.
To you I come,
before you I stand,
sinful and sorrowful.
O Mother of the Word incarnate,
despise not my petitions,
but in your mercy hear and answer me. Amen.

MEMORARE

Mary's Prayer

My soul magnifies the Lord,
and my spirit rejoices in God, my Savior,
for he has looked with favor on the lowliness of his
      servant.
Surely, from now on all generations will call me
      blessed;
for the Mighty One has done great things for me,
and holy is his name.
His mercy is for those who fear him
from generation to generation.
He has shown strength with his arm;
he has scattered the proud in the thoughts of their
      hearts.
He has brought down the powerful from their
      thrones,
and lifted up the lowly;
he has filled the hungry with good things,
and sent the rich away empty.
He has helped his servant Israel,
in remembrance of his mercy,
according to the promise he made to our ancestors,
to Abraham and to his descendents forever.

LUKE 1:46–55 (THE MAGNIFICAT)

Prayers of the Rosary

The Hail Mary
Hail Mary, full of grace, the Lord is with thee;
blessed art thou among women and blessed
is the fruit of thy womb, Jesus.
Holy Mary, Mother of God, pray for us sinners,
now and at the hour of our death. Amen.

The Our Father
Our Father, Who art in heaven,
hallowed be Thy name. Thy kingdom come;
Thy will be done on earth as it is in heaven.
Give us this day our daily bread;
and forgive us our trespasses,
as we forgive those who trespass against us.
And lead us not into temptation;
but deliver us from evil. Amen.

The Glory Be
Glory be to the Father, and to the Son, and to the
      Holy Spirit.
As it was in the beginning, is now,
and ever shall be, world without end. Amen.

The Mysteries of the Rosary

The Joyful Mysteries
   The Annunciation
   The Visitation
   The Nativity
   The Presentation
   The Finding of Jesus in the Temple

The Sorrowful Mysteries
   The Agony in the Garden
   The Scourging of Jesus
   The Crowning with Thorns
   The Carrying of the Cross
   The Crucifixion

The Glorious Mysteries
   The Resurrection
   The Ascension
   The Descent of the Holy Spirit
   The Assumption
   The Coronation of Our Lady

Apostles' Creed

I believe in God, the Father almighty,
    creator of heaven and earth,
I believe in Jesus Christ, his only son, our Lord.
    He was conceived by the power of the Holy Spirit
    and born of the Virgin Mary.
He suffered under Pontius Pilate, was crucified,
    died, and was buried.
He descended to the dead.
On the third day he rose again.
He ascended into heaven,
    and is seated at the right hand of the Father.
He will come again to judge the living and the dead.
I believe in the Holy Spirit,
    the holy catholic Church,
    the communion of saints,
    the forgiveness of sins,
    the resurrection of the body,
    and the life everlasting. Amen.

Nicene Creed

We believe in one God,
the Father, the Almighty,
maker of heaven and earth,
of all that is seen and unseen.
We believe in one Lord, Jesus Christ,
the only Son of God,
eternally begotten of the Father,
God from God, Light from Light,
true God from true God,
begotten, not made, one in Being with the Father.
Through him all things were made.
For us and for our salvation
he came down from heaven:
by the power of the Holy Spirit
he was born of the Virgin Mary, and became man.
For our sake he was crucified under Pontius Pilate;
he suffered, died, and was buried.
On the third day he rose again in fulfillment of the
        Scriptures:
he ascended into heaven
and is seated at the right hand of the Father.
He will come in glory to judge the living and the dead
and his kingdom will have no end.
We believe in the Holy Spirit,
the Lord, the giver of Life,

who proceeds from the Father and the Son.
With the Father and the Son he is worshiped and
    glorified.
He has spoken through the Prophets.
We believe in one holy catholic and apostolic Church.
We acknowledge one baptism for the forgiveness of
    sins.
We look for the resurrection of the dead,
and the life of the world to come. Amen.

A Meditation on the Stations of the Cross

Let us behold what care and pains our loving Lord
hath taken of our salvation;
Let us learn to travail courageously
and like devout and holy pilgrims
to follow his steps,
who hath left us an example
of his blessed life and passion.

JAN PASCHA

The Fourteen Stations of the Cross

The First Station:
Jesus is condemned to death on the cross

The Second Station:
Jesus accepts his cross

The Third Station:
Jesus falls the first time

The Fourth Station:
Jesus meets his sorrowful mother

The Fifth Station:
Simon of Cyrene helps Jesus carry his cross

The Sixth Station:
Veronica wipes the face of Jesus

The Seventh Station:
Jesus falls the second time

The Eighth Station:
Jesus meets and speaks to the woman of Jerusalem

The Ninth Station:
Jesus falls the third time

The Tenth Station:
Jesus is stripped of his garments

The Eleventh Station:
Jesus is nailed to the cross

The Twelfth Station:
Jesus dies on the cross

The Thirteenth Station:
Jesus is taken down from the cross

The Fourteenth Station:
Jesus is placed in the tomb

The Seven Last Words

1. *Father, forgive them; for they do not know what they are doing (Luke 23:34).*

You are hanging upon the cross. You nailed Yourself to it....Those who prepared all this for You stand there beneath the cross....They stand around. They laugh.... But you said: "Father, forgive them, for they know not what they do."...Where in all Your tortured and tormented soul did You find a place for words like these?

2. *Truly, I tell you, today you will be with me in Paradise (Luke 23:43).*

You are now in the agony of death. Your heart is filled to the brim with anguish, and yet You still have a place in that heart for the sufferings of another.

3. *Woman, here is your son....[Son, here is] your Mother (John 19:26).*

Even here in Your agony Your love is quick to express the tenderness which in this world every son feels for his mother. And through Your death even the tender, precious things of our world such as this are consecrated and sanctified, these things which make the heart gentle and the earth beautiful.

4. *My God, my God, why have you forsaken me?*
    (Matthew 27:46).

In this night of the senses and of the spirit, in this desert that consumes everything in Your heart, Your soul is still in prayer. The dreadful wasteland of a heart devastated by suffering becomes in You a solitary call to God.

5. *I am thirsty (John 19:28).*

You thirsted for me. You thirsted after my love and my salvation: as the deer thirsts for the spring, so does my soul thirst for You.

6. *It is finished (John 19:30).*

The end is Your fulfillment. For whoever comes to the end in love and fidelity has reached fulfillment. Your failure is Your triumph.

7. *Father, into your hands I commend my spirit*
    (Luke 23:46).

You let Yourself be taken from Yourself. You give Yourself over with confidence into those gentle, invisible hands. We who are weak in faith and fearful of our own selves experience those hands as the sudden, grasping, merciless, stifling grip of blind fate and of death. But You know that they are the hands of the Father.

KARL RAHNER

The Scriptural Stations

The First Station:
The agony of Jesus in the Garden of Olives

The Second Station:
The betrayal and arrest of Jesus

The Third Station:
The Sanhedrin condemns Jesus

The Fourth Station:
Peter denies Jesus

The Fifth Station:
Pilate condemns Jesus to the cross

The Sixth Station:
Jesus is scourged and crowned with thorns

The Seventh Station:
Jesus is mocked by the soldiers and given his cross

The Eighth Station:
Simon the Cyrenian helps Jesus carry his cross

The Ninth Station:
Jesus meets the women of Jerusalem

The Tenth Station:
Jesus is crucified

The Eleventh Station:
Jesus promises paradise to the penitent criminal

The Twelfth Station:
Jesus speaks to his mother and to his disciple

The Thirteenth Station:
Jesus dies on the cross

The Fourteenth Station:
The burial of Jesus

The Fifteenth Station:
Jesus rises from the dead

Favorite Patron Saints

Saint Francis of Assisi
Patron of animals and birds

Saint Jude Thaddeus
Patron of lost causes

Saint Thérèse of Lisieux
Patroness of missionaries and florists

Saint Anthony of Padua
Patron of lost articles

Saint Margaret of Antioch
Patroness of pregnancy and birth

Saint Joseph
Patron of fatherhood and families

Saint Mary
Patroness of motherhood

Saint Monica
Patroness of the widowed

Saint Valentine
Patron of love

Saint Patrick
Patron of Ireland

Saint Cecilia
Patroness of musicians

Saint Martin de Porres
Patron of racial harmony and social justice

Saint Nicholas
Patron of children

Saint Genevieve
Patroness of disaster

Saint Michael the Archangel
Patron of soldiers

Saint Thomas the Apostle
Patron of architects and builders

Saint Mary Magdalene
Patroness of repentant sinners

Saint Thomas Aquinas
Patron of students and scholars

Saint Clare of Assisi
Patroness of television

Saint Blaise
Patron of sore throats

Saint Teresa of Avila
Patroness of Spain and headaches

Saint Frances Cabrini
Patron of immigrants

Saint Vincent de Paul
Patron of charitable giving

Home

Night

Lord Jesus Christ,
you are the gentle moon and joyful stars,
that watch over the darkest night.
You are the source of all rest,
calming troubled hearts,
and bringing sleep to weary bodies.
You are the sweetness that fills our mind with quiet
joy,
and can turn the worst nightmares into dreams of
heaven.
May I dream of your sweetness,
rest in your arms,
be at one with your Father,
and be comforted in the knowledge
that you always watch over me.

DESIDERIUS ERASMUS

Gravities

High-riding kites appear to range quite freely
Though reined by strings, strict and invisible.
The pigeon that deserts you suddenly
Is heading home, instinctively faithful.

Lovers with barrages of hot insult
Often cut off their nose to spite their face.
Endure a hopeless day, declare their guilt,
Re-enter the native port of their embrace.

Blinding in Paris, for party-piece
Joyce named the shops along O'Connell Street
And on Iona Colmcille sought ease
By wearing Irish mould next to his feet.

SEAMUS HEANEY

A Prayer for Each Day

You have no need of our praise,
yet our desire to thank you is itself your gift.
Our prayer of thanksgiving adds nothing to your
    greatness,
but makes us grow in your grace,
through Christ Jesus our Lord.

From a PREFACE FOR WEEKDAYS

Icons

An icon is like a window
looking out upon eternity.
Behind its two-dimensional surface
lies the garden of God,
which is beyond dimension or size.

HENRI J. M. NOUWEN

At the Close of Day

May God support us all the day long,
till the shadows lengthen
and the evening comes
and the busy world is hushed
and the fever of life is over
and our work is done—
then in mercy—
may God give us a safe lodging
and a holy rest
and peace at last.

ATTRIBUTED TO JOHN HENRY NEWMAN

Landings Prayer

Lord, let me welcome all my sisters and brothers
with the arms of Christ.
May I listen to their stories
with the openness of Christ.
And may I embrace them
with the Love of Christ.
Through my hospitality,
may they once more
call our church their home. Amen.

RICHARD CHILSON, C.S.P.

Appendix I: Prayerful Contributors

St. Thomas Aquinas (1225–74): Thomas was a member of the Dominican order and a teacher at the University of Paris. His many works on theology influenced the thinking of the church for centuries after his death. Thomas also wrote hymns and meditations that have been frequently used in the prayer of the church.

Clement of Alexandria (third century, exact dates unknown): A cultured Greek scholar who spent much of his life in Egypt, Clement was noted as a mystic as well as a theologian. Third-century Alexandria was a center of Christian life, and Clement wrote many works encouraging seekers to become Christian.

St. Francis of Assisi (1182–1226): Francis is one of the most beloved of saints. As a young adult he renounced a life of comfort and gathered about him a group of men dedicated to a life of poverty and service to the poor. He loved poetry and music and enjoyed the beauty of nature, viewing all created things as his brothers and sisters.

St. Teresa of Avila (1515–82): Born in Spain, this beautiful and vivacious woman entered the Carmelite order against the wishes of her family. She devoted her many talents to the spiritual reform of the houses of sisters under her leadership. Teresa wrote many works detailing how to grow spiritually. Perhaps the most widely read of them is *The Interior Castle*.

Hans Urs von Balthasar (1905–88): Balthasar was a Swiss priest who studied literature and the arts as well as theology. He saw the appreciation of beauty as a way to contemplate God.

St. Bernard of Clairvaux (1090–1153): Bernard became the abbot of a monastery when he was twenty-five years old. He wrote many works on prayer and the monastic life. He was a key teacher in the development of a monastic spirituality within the Catholic Church.

Desiderius Erasmus (1466–1536): spent most of his life in Amsterdam, where he was a scholar of literature and scripture. He was a close friend of St. Thomas More and other leading thinkers. Through his writings he attacked religious abuses and hoped to spark a reform of the church.

Gerard Manley Hopkins (1844–88): Hopkins spent most of his life as a teacher in England and Ireland. His poetry was largely published after his death. He was one of the most creative and imaginative poets in the history of the English language. His poetry demonstrates his sharp eye and contemplative sensibility.

Thomas Merton (1915–68): Merton spent twenty-seven years as a monk at the Trappist monastery of Gethsemani, where he was known as Father Louis. His account of his decision to enter monastic life, *The Seven Storey Mountain*, has become one of the most widely read spiritual memoirs of all time. In subsequent years he wrote numerous books on prayer and was particularly interested in the close connection between social justice and a contemplative life.

John Henry Newman (1801–90): Newman spent the first half of his life as a member of the Church of England. His sermons and writings as the Anglican Rector of St. Mary's Church near Oxford were enormously influential. After a long period of study and struggle he became a Roman Catholic in 1843 and was ordained a priest four years later. He wrote about the development of his thought and the reasons for his conversion in his book *Apologia Pro Vita Sua* ("A Defense/Explanation of My Life"). He was created a cardinal in 1879.

Henri J. M. Nouwen (1930–99): Nouwen was born in the Netherlands but lived for many years in the United States. He was a priest, psychologist, university professor and author of spiritual memoirs and works on prayer. He spent his later years living and working in the L'Arche community founded by Jean Vanier.

Karl Rahner (1904–84): Rahner was a Jesuit priest who taught at universities in Germany and Austria. He was one of the most significant Catholic thinkers of the twentieth century.

Appendix II: Landings

Prayers for the Road Home: Signposts for Reclaiming Your Faith developed out of *Landings,* a process for welcoming returning Catholics to the church.

Landings is a ministry developed by Paulist Father Jac Campbell. The Paulist Fathers are a religious community of priests who have made reconciliation a keystone of their ministry since their founding in 1858. Beginning in Seattle in 1987 and later extending through the United States and Canada, *Landings* provides a welcoming experience through structured sessions, opportunities to share personal stories, occasions to share and witness to faith, personal and group prayer, and an invitation to reconciliation. The *Landings* format has been very successful in helping returning Catholics take another look at their faith.

A Special Word for *Landings* Participants

For those of you who are part of a *Landings* group, this booklet of prayer is offered as a way to help you with your private prayer time during your *Landings* weeks as well as with two *Landings* tasks.

At least once, during the weekly sessions, you will be given an opportunity to prepare the opening prayer time for your group. The main prayer–planning sheet remains in your *Landings Participant's Manual*. These prayers, some traditional, others modern, in whatever way you choose to use them, may evoke memories, spur imagination or simply help you get started in your own creative process of planning the prayer. Try to connect your prayer to the contemporary theme of the week. For instance, if the topic of the week is Jesus, plan your prayer around Jesus. If the topic is baptism, the prayer and materials used would relate to that sacrament.

In any case, all group members are invited to prepare weekly remarks for the appropriate contemporary Catholic theme. Consequently, we arranged the prayers, poems and excerpts under categories that roughly reflect the weekly topics of the *Landings* program. Spending a little time amid the wisdom of others is an excellent way to open a path into your own heart and soul.

Traditional texts that are still in use will help bring you up to date as well as evoke memories of earlier years. Others find contemporary words and songs a refreshing addition to their prayer lives.

Use and enjoy what is good for you and do not worry about the rest. Catholics comprise an enormous, wonderfully old spiritual family who boast a level of variety so extravagant it must be divinely inspired. Be yourself. After billions and billions of years of practice, you represent today's finest divine handiwork.

A Final Word of Gratitude

Two delightful surprises from my work with *Landings* include the enthusiasm with which people in remarkably different parish venues speak of the process. Again and again I hear "Father Jac, we just love *Landgins!*" Not many parish efforts are heralded that way.

A second surprise: Healing flows through families and parishes like new river branches. Among *Landings* graduates in Gig Harbor, Washington, who number about a hundred, my friend Mary returned. Since then, her children have been baptized, her sister came back, her husband joined the church and she leads her own group.

In that same parish another couple, originally from Maine, returned. Since then, they've welcomed back their children, their children's children and, last time I visited, a friend of their grandchildren was in the process of joining the parish.

Rather than single out anyone in particular for helping our ministry grow the way it has grown, I am simply grateful we could all cooperate with the grace of the Holy Spirit, in our own time and in our own age.

We dedicate this little prayer book to Mrs. Frances Sweeney and to all the parents who have prayed for our spiritual, physical and mental well-being. Mrs. Sweeney's son, Father Frank Sweeney, C.S.P., is our director of research. She died while we were working on this text.

Finally, as Jennifer Powers Fitzgerald said: "Sometimes, late in the day, when you want to write a little more, begin another project, do just one more thing, it is good to listen to your soul say: I think I've done enough today."

JAC CAMPBELL, C.S.P
Boston, Massachusetts
1 January 2001

Prayers Used in Text

Page 17   "Comfort in God's Care," Isaiah 40:1–2, 10–11.

Page 21   "Tidings of Great Joy," Preface for Advent II, in *The Sacramentary of the Roman Missal* (New York: Catholic Book Publishing Co., 1985), p. 374. (Subsequent citations of *The Sacramentary* refer to this work.)

Page 22   "God Becomes Flesh," Preface for Christmas I, in *The Sacramentary*, p. 378.

Page 23   "Recognizing Christ in Christmas," Preface for Christmas II, in *The Sacramentary,* p. 380.

Page 24   "Christ Is for All People," Preface for the Feast of the Epiphany, in *The Sacramentary*, p. 384.

Page 25   "Living Lent," Preface for Lent I, in *The Sacramentary*, p. 388.

Page 26   "Prayer before a Crucifix." Basil Doyle, C.S.P., in *Your Mass in Rhythmed Reading*, p. 70.

Page 27   "Easter Hymn," Taken from a much longer hymn dating from the fifth or sixth century (trans. J. M. Neale [1818–1866]). Cited in Gabe Huck, *Teach Me to Pray* (New York: Sadlier, 1981), p. 93.

Page 28   "The Joy of Easter," Preface for Easter IV, in *The Sacramentary*, p. 420.

Page 29   "An Open Heart," Brian Andreas.

Page 30   "Soul of Christ" ("Anima Christi"), a fourth-century prayer, translated by John Henry Newman, cited in Huck, *Teach Me to Pray*, p. 103.

Page 33   "The Gift of the Holy Spirit," Preface for the Holy Spirit II, in *The Sacramentary*, p. 482.

Page 34   "Come, Holy Ghost" ("Veni Creator Spiritus"), Text attr. to Robanus Maurus (776–856). Trans. by Edward Caswall (1814–78). Music: Louis Tambillotte, S.J. (1796–1855).

Page 36   "Come, Thou Holy Spirit" ("Veni Sancte Spiritus"), cited in Huck, *Teach Me to Pray,* p. 94.

Page 38   "Prayer to the Holy Spirit," taken from "Prayer before Mass, No. 56," in *The New St. Basil Hymnal*. Courtesy of the Basilian Fathers, Toronto.

Page 39   "A Prayer for Unity among Christians," Preface for Christian Unity, in *The Sacramentary*, p. 524.

Page 43   "Gather Us In," hymn by Marty Haugen (Chicago, Ill.: GIA Publications, 1982).

Page 44   "Christ's Body," Teresa of Avila (1515–82), cited in Jane Redmont, *When in Doubt, Sing* (New York: HarperCollins, 1999), p. 382.

Page 45   "Giving Thanks for the Saints," Preface for
           Holy Men and Women I, in *The Sacramen-
           tary*, p. 510.

Page 46   "Faithfulness, Not Performance," Thomas
           Merton, in *Thoughts in Solitude: Reflections
           on the Spiritual Life and the Love of Soli-
           tude* (Garden City, New York: Double-
           day/Image, 1968), p. 81.

Page 47   "Prayer for Guidance," "Lord, I have
           Time," by Michel Quoist, in *Prayers*, trans-
           lated by Agnes M. Forsyth and Anna Marie
           De Commaille (New York: Sheed and
           Ward, 1963), p. 97.

Page 48   "Prayer When Visiting a Church," Preface
           for the Dedication of a Church I, in *The
           Sacramentary*, p. 1140.

Page 49   "Inner Awareness," from Ephesians 1:18
           (New English Bible translation).

Page 53   "God's Mercy Is without Limit," taken
           from "Don't Think God Is Trying to
           Catch You," by Thomas Merton, from
           "Some Predisposition for Prayer," a con-
           ference on prayer (source: Thelma Hall).
           Cited in Redmont, *When in Doubt, Sing*,
           p. 25.

Page 54   "Prayer for Peace," attributed to St. Francis
           of Assisi (thirteenth century), from Huck,
           Teach Me to Pray, p. 118.

Page 55   "Wonder in the Presence of God," a tradi-
           tional hymn "Adoro Te," by Thomas
           Aquinas (thirteenth century), translated
           by Gerard Manley Hopkins. From Huck,
           Teach Me to Pray, p. 102.

Page 56   "The Food of Life," Preface for the Holy
           Eucharist II, in *The Sacramentary*, p. 468.

Page 57   "Peace Is Flowing Like a River," Rev.
           Cary Landry (North American Liturgy
           Resources, 1975).

Page 58   "Recognizing Christ in the Breaking of the
           Bread," Luke 24:13–16, 28–31a.

Page 59   "Traditional Hymn before the Eucharist"
           ("Tantum Ergo"), cited in Huck, *Teach Me
           to Pray*, p. 104.

Page 60   "Prayer of Silence," from "In Silence," in
           Quoist, *Prayers*.

Page 63   "Forgiveness," from "God Forgives You,"
           in *A New Zealand Prayer Book* (Church of
           the Province of New Zealand).

Page 64   "Love without Judgment," John 8:3–11.

Page 65   "Sorrow for Sin," traditional act of contri-
           tion for sins, in *Outlines of the Catholic
           Faith—Teachings, Beliefs, Practices, Prayers*
           (St. Paul, Minn.: The Leaflet Missal Com-
           pany, 1995), p. 76.

Page 82   "Prayer for Serenity," Reinhold Niebuhr
          (1892–1971), cited in Redmont, *When in
          Doubt, Sing*, p. 100.

Page 83   "Let Nothing Trouble You," Teresa of
          Avila (1515–82), ("Nada Te Turbe"), cited
          in Redmont, *When in Doubt, Sing*, p. 100.

Page 84   "The Communion of All the Saints," Pref-
          ace for All Saints, in *The Sacramentary*, p.
          514.

Page 85   "The Apostles, Our Protectors and
          Guides," Preface for the Feasts of the
          Apostles, in *The Sacramentary*, p. 500.

Page 86   "A Reflection on Doing God's Work," John
          Henry Newman, cited in Albert Weidner,
          Praying with John Cardinal Newman
          (Winona, Minn.: St. Mary's Press, 1997),
          p. 65.

Page 88   "Pray Always," Clement of Alexandria,
          "The Christian prays while walking...."

Page 91   "For the Angels," Preface for the Angels, in
          The Sacramentary, p. 492.

Page 92   "The Dead Will Rise," 1 Thessalonians
          4:16–18.

Page 93   "Prayer of Thanksgiving."

Page 94   "The Strife is O'er," text: *Finita iam sunt
          praelia* (Latin, twelfth century), trans.
          Francis Pott (1832–1909); music: Giovanni

da Palestrinea (1525–94). Adapted by W. H. Monk (1823–89).

Page 95   "The Dead," in Doyle, *Your Mass in Rhythmed Reading*, p. 62.

Page 96   "Farewell to One Who Has Died," from "Final Commendation, Invitation to Prayer," in *The Order of Christian Funerals* (Prepared by International Commission on English in the Liturgy. Collegeville, Minn.: Liturgical Press, 1998), p. 89.

Page 97   "In Hope of the Resurrection," based on "In Paradisum."

Page 98   "After a Death," from "Song of Farewell," in *The Order of Christian Funerals*, p. 90.

Page 101   "Devotion to the Saints Today," from "Every Authentic Witness," Dogmatic Constitution on the Church, No. 50, in *The Documents of Vatican II*, Walter M. Abbott, ed. (New York: America Press, 1966).

Page 103   "The Gift of the Saints," Hans Urs von Balthasar, in *The von Balthasar Reader* (New York: Crossroad Publishing Company, 1982).

Page 104   "What Makes a Saint?" Kenneth L. Woodward, in *Making Saints* (New York: Simon and Schuster, 1990).

Page 105   "Prayer to the Blessed Mother" ("Memo-
           rare"), attributed to St. Bernard of Clair-
           vaux (1090–1153), in Huck, *Teach Me to
           Pray*, p. 107.

Page 106   "Mary's Prayer," Luke 1:46–55 (the Mag-
           nificat), in Doyle, *Your Mass in Rhythmed
           Reading* p. 74.

Page 107   "Prayers of the Rosary," in Therese John-
           son Borchard, *Our Catholic Devotions*
           (New York: Crossroad, 1998), p. 32.

Page 108   "The Mysteries of the Rosary," in Bor-
           chard, *Our Catholic Devotions*, p. 24.

Page 109   "Apostles' Creed," in *The Sacramentary*, p.
           369.

Page 110   "Nicene Creed," in *The Sacramentary*, p.
           368.

Page 112   "A Meditation on the Stations of the
           Cross," from Jan Pascha, *The Spiritual Pil-
           grimage*, cited in Borchard, *Our Catholic
           Devotions,* p. 33.

Page 113   "The Fourteen Stations of the Cross," in
           Borchard, *Our Catholic Devotions*, pp.
           38–39.

Page 115   "The Seven Last Words," from Karl Rah-
           ner, S.J., *Prayers for a Lifetime* (New York:
           Crossroad, 1995), cited in Borchard, *Our
           Catholic Devotions*, pp. 41–42.

Page 117   "The Scriptural Stations," Pope John Paul II, cited in Borchard, *Our Catholic Devotions*, pp. 45–46.

Page 119   "Favorite Patron Saints," cited in Borchard, *Our Catholic Devotions*, pp. 103–4.

Page 125   "Night," Desiderius Erasmus (1469–1536).

Page 126   "Gravities," Seamus Heaney, in *Poems 1965–1975* (New York: Noonday Press, Farrar, Straus and Giroux, 1980), p. 31.

Page 127   "A Prayer for Each Day," Preface for Weekdays IV, in *The Sacramentary*, p. 452.

Page 128   "Icons," in Henri J. M. Nouwen, *Behold the Beauty of the Lord: Praying with Icons* (South Bend, Ind.: Ave Maria Press, 1987), p. 137.

Page 129   "At the Close of Day," prayer attributed to John Henry Newman (1801–90).

Page 130   "Landings Prayer," by Richard Chilson, C.S.P., Landings/Connections—Paulist Reconciliation Ministries, Boston, Mass.